Age of
Aquarius
You and Astrology

By Franklyn M. Branley and Leonard Kessler

A Book of Astronauts for You
A Book of Flying Saucers for You
A Book of Mars for You
A Book of Moon Rockets for You
A Book of Outer Space for You
A Book of Planet Earth for You
A Book of Planets for You
A Book of Satellites for You
A Book of Stars for You
A Book of the Milky Way Galaxy for You
A Book of Venus for You
Age of Aquarius: You and Astrology

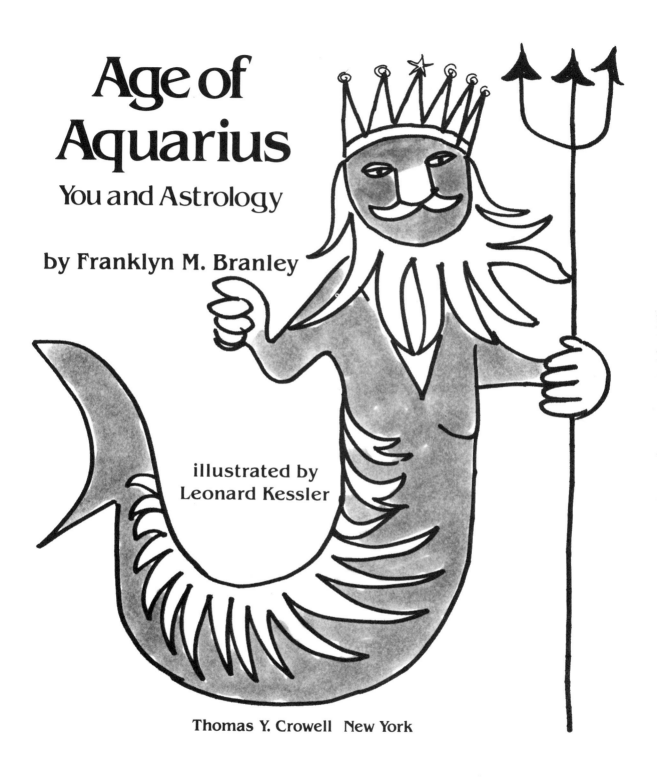

Age of Aquarius
You and Astrology

by Franklyn M. Branley

illustrated by
Leonard Kessler

Thomas Y. Crowell New York

Age of Aquarius: You and Astrology
Text copyright © 1979 by Franklyn M. Branley
Illustrations copyright © 1979 by Leonard Kessler
All rights reserved. Printed in the United States of America. No part of this book may be used
or reproduced in any manner whatsoever without written permission except in the case of
brief quotations embodied in critical articles and reviews. For information address Thomas Y.
Crowell, 10 East 53rd Street, New York, N. Y. 10022. Published simultaneously in Canada
by Fitzhenry & Whiteside Limited, Toronto.
Designed by Joyce Hopkins
FIRST EDITION

Library of Congress Cataloging in Publication Data
Branley, Franklyn Mansfield, 1915–
    Age of Aquarius: you and astrology.

    Bibliography: p.
    Includes index.
    SUMMARY: Basic information about the roots
of astrology and the beliefs of astrologers today, with
directions for casting your own horoscope.
    1. Astrology–Juvenile literature. [1. Astrology]
I. Kessler, Leonard P., 1920– II. Title.
BF1708.1.B72 1979   133.5   78–22511
ISBN 0–690–03987–5
ISBN 0–690–03988–3 lib. bdg.

Astrologers believe that our lives are tied closely to the planets and the stars. There are good planets, they believe, and bad ones. If the good planets were in the sky when you were born, you're lucky. If the wrong ones were there, that's not so good. But things may get better later on, for the planets will move into new positions. Astrologers say that the planets are very important in our lives, as also are certain signs in the sky.

Do you know what your sign is? Do you know if you are an Aries or a Taurus, a Gemini or a Libra? If, for example, your birthday comes between July 23 and August 22, you are a Leo. *Leo* is the Latin word for lion. People who believe in astrology say that anyone born under the sign of the lion will be like the king of the beasts.

He will be brave and will work hard. At times he will be playful, but he can also "show his claws" and roar when he's angry.

Find where the date of your birth falls in the descriptions of the signs given below, and then read what the astrologers believe you are like.

March 21–April 19
ARIES,
the ram

A ram is a male sheep that butts other sheep with his horns. So you are a pusher, you get things done. You make many friends, and enjoy being a leader. You like to try out new ideas, and are good in many different kinds of sports.

April 20–May 20
TAURUS,
the bull

Like a bull, a Taurus is steady and strong. You do things yourself, and do not depend on other people. You are slow to anger, but people get out of your way when you are angry. The chances are that you are healthy and are solidly built. You are a hard worker at school and also at home. Like a bull, you like to eat. You have a good business head and work well with finances.

May 21–June 20
GEMINI,
the twins

A Gemini, like twins, often does two or more things at the same time. You are changeable; you go easily and often from one friend to another, from one sport to another, or one hobby to another.

You are active; you like to go places rather than stay at home. You are good at jobs that require handwork, such as model making, sewing, and piano playing. The double nature of your interests may cause you to start more things than you can finish.

June 21–July 22
CANCER,
the crab

Like a crab, if you are a Cancer you keep to yourself. You are stubborn, and curious. You sit back and study people, so you know them very well. Travel is only of passing interest, for a Cancer would rather be at home. Like a crab, you hold onto things and so have money in the bank. You are a collector, and not much interested in sports, unless they have something to do with water, such as swimming, fishing, and skin diving.

July 23–August 22
LEO,
the lion

You have already read something about a Leo. In addition, you are very active and work hard to excel in whatever you do. You may show off at times, but you do not need to because you are really able to do things well. You like clothes and adornments such as rings and necklaces. Also, you try everything, even though sometimes what you try may prove risky. A Leo would make a good actor or producer; or a good leader, for example, a class president.

5

August 23–September 22
VIRGO,
the virgin

A Virgo likes to find things out for himself. You have only a few friends, but they are good ones. You like good music and plays, and enjoy them more than rock and roll; your favorite sports are hunting, riding, and climbing. You are a good student, you read a lot, and though you enjoy a joke, you smile rather than laugh loudly.

September 23–October 23
LIBRA,
the scales

A Libra is a weigher, a balancer, a good umpire devoted to fair play, and interested in doing things right. You work hard and long at times, then relax and do nothing. You are apt to eat and get fat, and then diet and get thin. You are well liked, and are always helping others. Team sports are most appealing to you, and your hobbies are apt to include raising fish or animals, designing clothes, or doing experiments in chemistry or other scientific fields. One problem is that as a Libra you are unable to make up your mind easily because you can see both sides of an argument.

October 24–November 22
SCORPIO,
the scorpion

A Scorpio is determined. You work toward a goal, and nothing can stop you or change your mind. You like privacy; you are very comfortable by yourself. You make decisions easily, and have energy and vitality to carry out your plans. You are inclined to be lean and sinewy and to enjoy sports where you compete against a clock or a record (pole-vaulting, for example) rather than against an opponent. You are successful in school and, in fact, in most everything you do.

November 23–December 21
SAGITTARIUS,
the archer

A Sagittarius is a sharp person, like an arrow. You make friends easily and like people so much that you can see no wrong in them. You are outgoing and so would make a good actor or singer, or a salesperson. Money is not important, except to be spread around and used. It passes through your fingers, yet you always seem to have some. You love to be active in clubs or wherever people are involved. You like to travel, but not alone.

December 22–January 19

CAPRICORN,
the goat

A Capricorn, like a goat, is surefooted. You pick your way carefully, and are eager and ambitious. Perhaps you work after school or on weekends to earn money. You are very practical and so are always prepared. You like doing something worthwhile; your hobbies are useful ones, such as cooking or repairing trains and other toys. You have hard muscles and make a good wrestler. You also have good health. Some Capricorns get so involved in following rules, and being practical, that they fail to participate in "fun" activities.

January 20–February 19
AQUARIUS,
the water bearer

An Aquarius is lucky, for you carry wisdom (the water in the jar). You change a lot, and sometimes are active with others and sometimes want to be alone. You are very liberal, and believe that people should do as they please. You like to help others, either with money or in a job. You like to solve puzzles, mysteries, and riddles. Being ordinary bothers you, for you would rather be different, lead the way.

February 20–March 20
PISCES,
the fishes

A Pisces is deep, like the ocean. Few people really know you. You change quickly from happy to sad, from active to inactive. You are good at adapting yourself to others: among quiet people, you are one of the most quiet; among active people, the most active. You are probably interested in art of some kind. In sports, swimming is your favorite. And you'll either be an actor or be in some trade related to water.

These are just a few of the things that astrologers believe they know about you when they find out what sign you were born under. In addition, your sign tells an astrologer which planets affect you the most, what your favorite colors are, what parts of your body are especially strong or weak, what metals you most resemble; for example, strong-willed like iron or flighty like quicksilver.

Why Astrology Began

Such ideas are not new. Astrology began thousands of years ago. Long before the birth of Christ, people called the Babylonians (and the Chaldeans before them) gazed into the sky. They watched the stars and planets and believed that they had strong effects on their lives.

The Babylonians lived in a river valley that lies east of the Mediterranean Sea. The valley is in a place that was called Mesopotamia (between the rivers) by the Greeks, and which we now call Iraq. The Babylonians built large cities. They grew crops and irrigated them by building canals. Artists made beautiful statues and designed pottery. The Babylonians developed a system of writing—cuneiform—and they learned how to keep a written record of events. Certain priests were advisors to the king. They used the stars and planets to forecast events in the life of the king. The priests started astrology.

The Babylonians, like many other ancient peoples, looked to their gods for help of all kinds. For example, they believed that one god or another was responsible for whatever happened. Suppose the king, his son, and members of the king's court were hunting. And suppose the son slipped and fell to his death in a deep canyon.

Why was it the king's son who fell and not someone else? It must be because a powerful god was punishing the king. He must have done something to displease the god. Ancient people did not believe in chance. There must be a reason for everything that happened. People wanted to know why they became sick, why there were floods and famines. They sought help in warfare, in planting crops and harvesting food. They always turned to the gods, for they believed there was a god who managed each separate part of their lives. All told, the Babylonians had four thousand gods.

The lives of the people were closely tied to the fortunes of the king. The king was but a notch below the gods; perhaps he was a god himself. It was important for him to communicate somehow with the gods. It was thought that the gods could warn him of a calamity such as an invasion of locusts, severe droughts or floods, an attack from an enemy. The king would thus be able to prepare for the future, and so protect his people.

Priests were important members of the king's court. It was through the priests that the gods could send messages about the future. One way of doing this was by using the livers of animals—goats, lambs, calves—that had been sacrificed to please the gods. The organ of the liver is filled with blood, and so it was regarded by the ancients as the seat of life itself, the center of all activity. Through observing the "signs" on a particular liver, the priest could enter into the mind of the god to whom the sacrifice was made. Then, since he knew the mind of the god, the priest also knew what the god might do.

Suppose the sacrifice had been made to Ninurta, the god of war. The priest would "read" markings on the liver that would foretell whether a battle would end in victory. The priest could read the liver because livers differ. A swollen liver generally meant increased harvests, but it could also mean a flood. Usually markings on the right side of the liver were favorable, while those on the left were unfavorable.

Whatever the signs on the liver might mean was learned from experience. Suppose a priest examined a liver and found a deep, straight mark on the right half. And suppose that after he had observed this mark, something favorable happened. Perhaps there was a rich harvest, and plenty of food for everyone. Whenever that mark was seen again by the priest, he would know what it meant. The god of harvest was foretelling that there would be food in large supply. Or if the sacrifice had been made to the god of war, the priest might decide that the god was telling the king to go ahead with his war plans. If the sacrifice was made to the god of life, that god might be letting the king know that he was to have a strong and healthy child.

The most important of all the four thousand Babylonian gods was Zu-en or Sin, the moon god that changed from night to night. The followers of Sin lived in the city of Ur, one of the most important of all ancient cities. The next most powerful god was the son of the moon, Shamash, the god of the sun. Each of the five planets that we can see without a telescope was also an important god. Sin (the moon), Shamash (the sun), Marduk (Jupiter), Ishtar (Venus), Ninib (Saturn), Nebo (Mercury), and Nergal (Mars) were the seven gods of the sky.

These heavenly gods were of special importance to the priests. They were the ones that affected most strongly the king's life and happiness, and through him the lives and happiness of all. These gods, who controlled the skies, brought sunshine and pleasant weather, without which there would be no crops. And the same gods brought rain; it fell from the heavens. It was important to treat the gods well, for the same gods could also cause destruction. They could flood the rivers. They could ruin crops with strong winds and violent storms. They could even cut the crops to pieces with hailstones.

The priests connected what occurred in the sky with what happened on earth. Sin and Shamash (the moon and the sun) moved smoothly and evenly across the sky. They produced law and order in the sky, and on the earth as well. The movements of the other gods (the planets) were not as smooth and regular. Their motion indicated to the priests that the planets were active; they were causing all kinds of events to occur on the earth—good harvests or bad, peace or warfare.

The task of the priests was to figure out which events in the heavens were connected with events on earth; for example, if two planets were close together, it might be the sign of the birth of a prince, or of a period of dry weather, or of a victory in battle. It could mean almost anything, depending upon what had previously happened when the same two planets were close together. The interpretations often included the bright stars in a constellation. For example, suppose in springtime Mars was seen to move toward an especially bright star. And suppose that about the same time, a prince was born. Ever afterward, the movement of Mars toward that star would be a good omen meaning a son was to be born to the royal family. Eclipses, too, were especially significant. All manner of events on earth, good and bad, that occurred during that time would be connected to the eclipse.

The priests kept a record of sky events and earthly occurrences. The priests' explanations were originally based upon memory, and later upon written records of what had taken place in the past. A victory in battle may have occurred when Jupiter and Mars were close together. From that time on, the priests believed that if a battle took place when Jupiter and Mars were close together it would end in victory, just as it had before.

The priests were giving explanations by relating one event to another, even though one had nothing to do with the other. For example, the full moon might have risen in a cloudy sky and so appeared orange-red. A day or so later, there may have been long, steady rain that saved the crops from drying out. Thereafter, an orange-red moon became a good omen—the gods were foretelling that the crops would be saved.

Babylonian priests, the early astrologers, were not involved with individuals. They were concerned with the influence of the gods upon the king. The king was all-important; whatever affected him was felt throughout the land. If the positions of the sun, moon, and planets indicated that the king was in favor with the gods, all his people would share in his good fortune. If the king was out of favor, calamities were likely to happen to everyone.

The priests were astronomers as well as astrologers. As astronomers they studied the motions of the sun, moon, and the visible planets, and they learned much about them. As astrologers they read the skies for meanings, meanings that would affect the fate of the king and so the fate of the entire kingdom.

How Astrology Spread

In Babylonia astrology was reserved for the king and the court. But in other lands, and at later times, the fate of individual persons was concerned. The trend started with the Egyptians, who broadened the importance of astrology to include not only the rulers but the masses of the people. The sun, moon, and stars played large parts in Egyptian religion. One of their principal gods was Ra, the sun god. (They had three different sun gods: Horus, god of the rising sun; Atmu, god of the setting sun; and most important, Ra, god of the noonday sun.) The Egyptians believed that the dead were reborn as different objects; they appeared in the sky as stars. The Egyptian sign for soul is *. You can see that it is closely related to ★, which is our present symbol for a star.

Egyptian priests knew about the positions of the stars and their motions. The Great Pyramid, built thousands of years ago, is lined up with what was at that time the North Star. The North Star has changed its position over the centuries. Today we know the rate of change, and so have a clue to when this pyramid was built. It turns out to be about 4700 B.C.

The Egyptians knew the skies well, and they believed that events in their lives were influenced by the stars. So did most other people of the ancient world. Among ancient people, the Greeks developed astrology most widely.

Much of modern astrology comes from the Greeks. The early Greeks learned their astrology from teachers who were brought to Greece from Babylonia. Much later, after it was well established, Greek astrology was written down by the Greek scholar Claudius Ptolemy, who lived in Egypt, in the city of Alexandria. At that time Egypt, along with many other countries, was ruled by the Greeks. Ptolemy was an observer of the sky. Some of the first sky maps and also lists of the stars were made by him. Two books written by Ptolemy became very famous. One of them was called the *Almagest* which means "the greatest." The book described the arrangement of the planets. Ptolemy said that the earth was at the center of them. It stood still, and all the planets, the sun and the moon and the stars circled about the earth. The viewpoint was incorrect, but it explained why the objects appeared to move as they did. Ptolemy included information about stars and star positions. For hundreds of years the information was valuable to navigators and to other watchers of the skies.

Ptolemy was an astronomer. He was also an astrologer. His

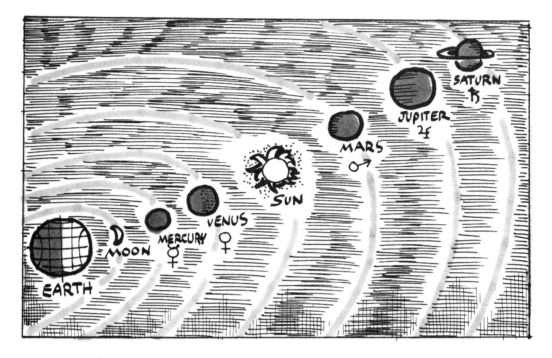

second famous book was called the *Tetrabiblos*. (*Tetra* means four, and *biblos* means books.) It was divided into the Four Books on the Influence of the Stars. Even today these works are used by astrologers; they contain most of the knowledge of astrology that we have today.

The Greeks were fascinated by fortune-telling of all kinds: by the lines in a person's hand, the way one's hair parted, one's appetite for certain foods. But their best way of telling one's fortune was to use the stars and planets. The Greeks changed Babylonian astrology in many ways. For example, they developed the horoscope. It is a chart of the positions of the planets and stars, and signs—called zodiacal signs—at the time of a person's birth.

The Babylonian astrologers made sky charts for the day of a

king's birth, and also for special times in his life. The Greeks made charts for everyone. Many people are born on the same day, and so it would seem that the stars should foretell the same future for each of them. But that obviously could not be so. The Greeks solved the problem by making charts not for entire days, but for a certain hour of the day, and even for a certain minute. They used the word *horoscope* for the chart, and for the meanings that they read from it. The word horoscope means "a look at the hour," the "hour" being the moment when a person is born.

At the same time that the Greeks were developing the horoscope, they were learning about botany and zoology, about astronomy, medicine, and anatomy. They grouped astrology along with these sciences.

The Greeks refined ancient beliefs in the special influence of each of the planets. They kept alive the Babylonian idea of associating each planet with a certain color. They also connected the planets to certain metals, and to parts of the body, as you see on page 32. They taught that this influence changed depending upon whether the planets were high in the sky, just rising, or setting at the moment when a person was born.

Interest in astrology was transferred from the Greeks to the Romans when the Roman legions defeated the Greek armies. But the takeover was not immediate, for the Romans were strong believers in the kind of fortune-telling that depended upon the behavior of birds, insects, and animals. These were the objects that foretold the future, they said. They also believed, as had the Babylonians, that the future could be told from a study of the organs of animals that had been sacrificed to one of their gods. At first, the idea that objects in the sky could determine the fortunes of a person did not make sense to them. However, toward the end of the second century B.C., astrology started to become popular throughout the lands of the Romans.

For many centuries Rome flourished, and so did astrology. The Romans spread their ideas over thousands of miles, all along the Mediterranean Sea. More and more people regulated their lives according to their horoscopes. Eventually the Roman Empire fell. Barbarians came out of the north. They attacked the Romans and defeated them. The barbarians destroyed books and ideas, including the ways the ancient priests had found to "read" the stars. People entered a period called the Dark Ages. For several hundred years, learning stopped. There were no schools, and people could neither read nor write. In their ignorance they came to believe more and more in fortune-telling by the birds and animals and magic, just as the early Romans had done. When there was thunder and lightning, the gods were angry; they were punishing the people for some wrong committed.

During the Dark Ages the Roman Catholic church was the preserver of knowledge. Whatever records remained were kept in the churches. And knowledge was passed from one priest to another. The church prohibited belief in magic. Astrology was therefore prohibited because it was a kind of magic; it was fortune-telling by the stars.

While astrology was becoming less important in Europe, it remained important in the Eastern world. In Arabia and as far east as India, for example, it was considered a science, just as the Greeks had thought it. Indeed, in Arabia there were only four sciences: arithmetic, geometry, the structure of the universe, and astrology.

During the Dark Ages in Europe, the Arabian world kept alive the writings of Ptolemy, including the *Tetrabiblos.* Around the year 1200 the Dark Ages ended, and the Arabs reintroduced astrology to Europe. Written records were translated into Latin, the language of scholars. The schools that were being revived often taught astrology.

Learning spread rapidly across Europe. People were interested in medicine and anatomy, and in astronomy. Sky observers were soon to learn the true movements of the sun, moon, and planets. Eventually Galileo was to see the phases of Venus and four of the 13 moons of Jupiter through his newly invented telescope.

And astrology reached a new level of importance. It was just as important to people of the sixteenth and seventeenth centuries as it had been to the Romans and the Greeks and Babylonians. Once more, kings would not make decisions without counsel of a court astrologer. To gain support from the ruler, astronomers had to practice astrology. Kings would not aid someone who simply made and studied maps of the sky, as astronomers did. But they would give all sorts of help to someone who could tell the king what was to happen in the future, as astrologers did.

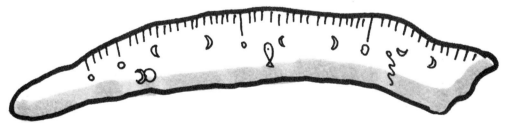

Most astronomers made horoscopes and used them to advise their kings. They had to. Many of them also believed strongly in the magic of astrology. Others made horoscopes for the kings not because they believed in the teachings, but because it was a way to support their work in astronomy.

The methods that these European astrologers used in making horoscopes had grown out of the astrology of ancient Babylonia, Greece, and Rome. And they are still used today.

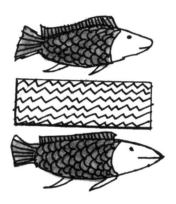

Signs in the Sky

As we saw earlier, there are twelve signs that an astrologer uses— Aries, Taurus, Leo, and so on. Each sign is assigned a region of the sky. The regions are connected, so altogether they make a belt that goes from west to east all across the sky.

Each sign has a symbol that represents it. We are not sure how these symbols originated, but they may well have come from ancient picture writing, as old as the Babylonians or older. You can find the modern symbol for your sign and also the ancient picture symbol in the list on page 29.

The twelve signs of astrology were probably started by the Babylonians. In addition to having many gods, the Babylonians worshiped all sorts of monstrous creatures. There was a bull with a man's head, dogs and goats with fishes' tails, wolves that foamed at the mouth, and scorpions with gigantic stingers. Altogether there were twelve monsters.

Gods must live somewhere. Ancient people, the Babylonians among them, believed that some of their gods lived in the trees or behind big rocks. Other gods might live in certain rooms of certain houses, or perhaps in bushes or inside certain animals. One of the best places for the gods to live was in the sky. From there, they could look down upon everyone. The homes of the twelve special creatures of the Babylonians were in the part of the sky through which moved their most important gods—Sin and Shamash (the moon and the sun).

The path of Sin and Shamash was called "the way of Anu," Anu being the king of the gods. It could be identified by thirty-six stars; the brightest twelve of them were the "chiefs." This region of the sky was observed constantly by the priests. For not only was it the path of Sin and Shamash, but it was the home of the other major gods—Marduk, Ishtar, Ninib, Nebo, and Nergal. These, you will recall, are the five planets that can be seen without a telescope—Jupiter, Venus, Saturn, Mercury, and Mars. Whenever we see these planets, they are close to "the way of Anu." Sometimes they are right in it. When the Greeks took up astrology, they adopted "the way of Anu," and many of the "signs" or creatures of the Babylonians. They changed others to creatures or objects of their own choosing. It turns out that of the twelve objects in the belt, eleven of them are identified as animals or people. The exception is Libra the Scales. Since there are so many "creatures" in the belt, the Greeks called it zodiakos—the belt of the animals. The Greek word for a living being or animal is *zoion*—you can see the same root in zoology (the study of animals), and of course in zoo (zoological park), an animal park.

The zodiac is the imaginary belt of the twelve signs that astrologers use to locate the sun, the moon, and the planets. (Also, it is the belt of twelve clusters of stars or constellations that bear the same names.) So, for example, there is the constellation of Aries the ram, Taurus the bull, and so on. The star groups do not look like a ram or a bull, but they do serve to identify each region in the sky.

Each of the planets moves along this region, as do the sun and the moon. Each passes from one of the twelve constellations, or signs, to another. The signs maintain the same order as the constellations, beginning with Aries, then Taurus, Gemini, Cancer, and the rest. Aries is number one. In the days of the Babylonians, the sun entered Aries in springtime. When that happened, the year began. It was a good time to start the year, because day and night were about the same length, seeds were planted, there was a revival of trees and plants that had been dormant during the winter. Also, Aries was a ram that was leader of the flock.

The first day of the year (to the Babylonians) came in March. (For centuries, New Year's Day came in March. In our own land it wasn't changed to January 1 until 1753.) Today, the ancient New Year's Day has become the first day of spring. In the time of the ancients, the sun was in Aries in March. Now it is in the constellation Pisces. For you and me, spring actually begins when the sun is in Pisces. The sun over the centuries has shifted its position. It is now in Pisces from March 14 to April 12. However, most astrologers distinguish between the sign and the constellation. They still make forecasts as though the sun had not shifted; as though the sun was in Aries for most of this time interval—just as it was a long time ago.

As the year goes by, the sun seems to move from sign to sign, from Sagittarius to Capricorn, to Aquarius, Pisces, and so on, all around the sky. The path the sun follows is important to astrologers. Your sign tells you where the sun was at the time of your birth. Some astrologers think the moon is very important in telling about the future. So its location at the time of your birth is something else that they like to find out. Also, most astrologers think the planets affect our lives. To them, it is necessary to know where the planets were when you were born. Or, if you will be making an important decision, the astrologer wants to find out in which signs the planets will be when you make that decision so you can be advised.

These locations are always changing. The planets move through one sign of the zodiac to another as they move around the sun. The solar system is quite flat; it is shaped more like a saucer than a ball. For this reason the planets are always close to the same line that the sun moves along. Each therefore is always in one of the twelve signs.

Astrologers believe that the planets rule certain signs. If at the moment of one's birth, a planet should happen to be in the sign of the zodiac that it rules, conditions connected with that sign would be especially strong. The chart below shows the signs of the zodiac and their ruling planets.

Sign of the Zodiac	Ruling Planet
Aries	Mars
Taurus	Venus
Gemini	Mercury
Cancer	Moon
Leo	Sun
Virgo	Mercury
Libra	Venus
Scorpio	Mars
Sagittarius	Jupiter
Capricorn	Saturn
Aquarius	Saturn
Pisces	Jupiter

You will notice that three of the planets—Uranus, Neptune, and Pluto—are not included. That is because they were not discovered until after the telescope had been invented. Uranus was discovered in 1781, only about two hundred years ago; Neptune was found sixty-five years later, in 1846; Pluto, the most recently discovered, was found in 1930.

Modern astrology is based upon Greek astrology; the ancients knew nothing about those three planets, so many astrologers pay no attention to them today. That is why we have left them out of the chart.

The five planets and the sun and the moon were considered to be seven special gods. They were so important to the ancients that each was given a day—a special day during which it was the supreme ruler. The days of the week and their ruling planets are listed here. (Their Old English names have also been included so that you can see how we arrived at the modern names for the days in English.)

Days of the Week

Day	Planet	Old English Name
Monday	Moon	Monan Daeg
Tuesday	Mars	Tiwes Daeg
Wednesday	Mercury	Wodnes Daeg
Thursday	Jupiter	Thunres Daeg
Friday	Venus	Frige Daeg
Saturday	Saturn	Saetern Daeg
Sunday	Sun	Sunnan Daeg

The order of the days—Monday, Tuesday, Wednesday, and so forth—was not accidental. The order of the planets was based on the time each planet needed to circle the earth. Saturn took the longest and therefore came first. Jupiter took the next longest, and so it was in second place. The sequence was Saturn, Jupiter, Mars, sun, Venus, Mercury, moon. It was the opposite of the order of their supposed distances from the earth, the moon being considered the nearest and Saturn the farthest. (See page 18.)

27

Each planet (god) was assigned its own day as shown on the list. While that planet ruled over the entire twenty-four-hour period, a different planet was assigned to each hour. It worked out this way: the day was named after whatever planet ruled during the first hour after sunrise. The next planet in order ruled the second hour, and so on, throughout the twenty-four hours.

For example, let us start with Saturday (Saturn's day). Saturn ruled over the entire day, but during the second hour Jupiter was especially important. During the third hour, the ruling planet was Mars; during the seventh hour, the moon. The eighth hour, it was Saturn again.

Count the planets in their sequential order, starting with Saturn and going to Jupiter, Mars, the sun, etc., and then start with Saturn again, until you reach twenty-four. That will be Mars, the ruler of the last hour of that day. The next object after Mars is the sun. So, twenty-four hours after Saturn's day begins, the sun will become the ruler; then it will be Sunday. Beginning with the sun, once again count along the list to twenty-four. That takes you to Mercury, the ruler of the last hour of Sunday. The following object is the moon. The next day is therefore Monday, and so on, for each of the seven days of the week.

Astrological Signs and Their Meanings

THE SIGNS AND THEIR SYMBOLS. Each of the twelve signs of the zodiac is identified by a symbol. We do not know how these symbols came into being. Probably they were derived from ancient picture writing that existed long before the Babylonians. The names of the signs, the symbols, and the ancient picture writing that may relate to them are shown below:

Sign	Symbol	Ancient Picture Writing
Aries	♈	
Taurus	♉	
Gemini	♊	
Cancer	♋	
Leo	♌	
Virgo	♍	
Libra	♎	
Scorpio	♏	
Sagittarius	♐	
Capricorn	♑	
Aquarius	♒	
Pisces	♓	

The chart on page 32 shows how the zodiac is divided into twelve different signs. Along with these signs and the planets, there are other clues—elements, parts of the body, colors—that are part of the chart. Later on, you will see how you can make your own horoscope, using this information.

THE PLANETS AND THEIR SYMBOLS. The planet Saturn was named after the god of time. This was because it was the slowest-moving of all the seven "planets" that the ancients could see. The symbol is a sickle, a reminder of the scythe carried by Father Time.

Mercury

Two serpents wound around a wand. This is the symbol of the wand carried by the god Mercury, the bearer of tidings and messages.

Venus

A hand mirror. It is proper that Venus the goddess of love and beauty should have a hand mirror.

Mars

Mars was the god of war. The symbol is supposed to represent a shield and a spear.

Jupiter

Jupiter was the king of the gods. The symbol is supposed to be a great thunderbolt.

Sun

The sun was considered perfect, and so it was represented by a circle standing alone. Later, a dot was added; it probably came from early maps of the solar system, which showed the sun moving around the earth.

Moon
The symbol, of course, represents how the moon appears during the crescent phase.

ELEMENTS. The ancients believed that the world was made of four basic substances—fire, earth, air, and water. Astrologers connected these elements with the signs of the zodiac. They began by assigning fire to Aries, earth to Taurus, and so on, around the twelve signs.

PARTS OF THE BODY. It was believed that a person's health was affected by the influence of the planets. Beginning with the head —the center that controlled all others—the various parts of the body were assigned to the different signs: the head to Aries, the neck to Taurus, shoulders and arms to Gemini, and so on—all around the zodiac—until the feet were reached.

FEMININE AND MASCULINE. Almost all living things are either feminine or masculine. Early astrologers believed that the signs should be divided in a similar way. Starting with Aries, which they termed masculine, the astrologers alternated the two. In this way Taurus the bull and Capricorn the goat became feminine, even though they are usually considered masculine. This contradiction did not bother ancient astrologers. Most modern astrologers, however, do not use these terms. Instead, they call masculine signs positive or electric, and feminine signs negative or magnetic.

COLORS. The Greek astrologers felt that certain colors were more important in a given horoscope than were other colors. A person born under Capricorn, for example, was partial to deep blue. The

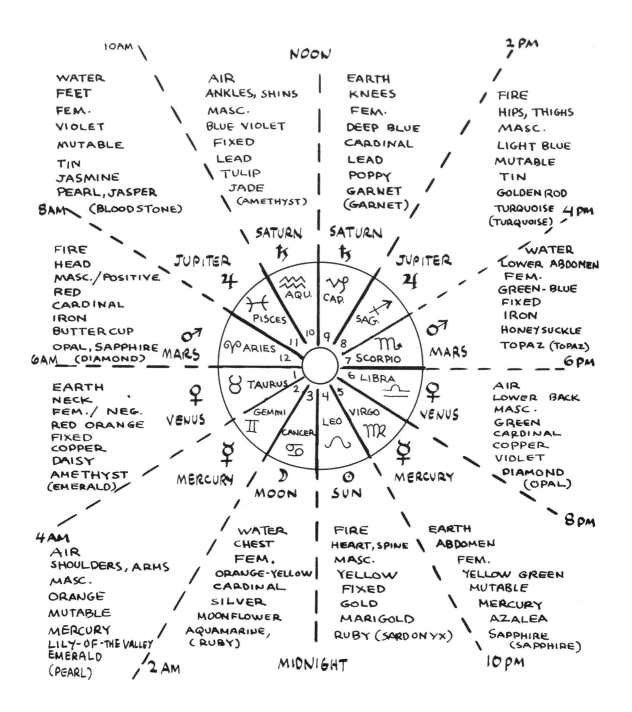

10AM

NOON

2PM

WATER
FEET
FEM.
VIOLET
MUTABLE
TIN
JASMINE
PEARL, JASPER
8AM   (BLOODSTONE)

AIR
ANKLES, SHINS
MASC.
BLUE VIOLET
FIXED
LEAD
TULIP
JADE
(AMETHYST)

EARTH
KNEES
FEM.
DEEP BLUE
CARDINAL
LEAD
POPPY
GARNET
(GARNET)

FIRE
HIPS, THIGHS
MASC.
LIGHT BLUE
MUTABLE
TIN
GOLDEN ROD
TURQUOISE 4PM
(TURQUOISE)

SATURN
♄

SATURN
♄

FIRE
HEAD
MASC./POSITIVE
RED
CARDINAL
IRON
BUTTERCUP
OPAL, SAPPHIRE
6AM   (DIAMOND)

JUPITER
♃

JUPITER
♃

WATER
LOWER ABDOMEN
FEM.
GREEN-BLUE
FIXED
IRON
HONEYSUCKLE
TOPAZ (TOPAZ)
6PM

MARS ♂

♒ AQU.
PISCES ♓
ARIES ♈
11 10
12

♑ CAP.
SAG. ♐
8
7 SCORPIO ♏
6 LIBRA ♎
9

♂ MARS

EARTH
NECK
FEM./NEG.
RED ORANGE
FIXED
COPPER
DAISY
AMETHYST
(EMERALD)

VENUS
♀

TAURUS ♉
GEMINI ♊
1
2
3 4 5
CANCER ♋
LEO ♌
VIRGO ♍
♍

♀
VENUS

AIR
LOWER BACK
MASC.
GREEN
CARDINAL
COPPER
VIOLET
DIAMOND
(OPAL)
8PM

MERCURY
☿

MOON
☽

SUN
☉

MERCURY
☿

4AM
AIR
SHOULDERS, ARMS
MASC.
ORANGE
MUTABLE
MERCURY
LILY-OF-THE VALLEY
EMERALD
(PEARL)   2AM

WATER
CHEST
FEM.
ORANGE-YELLOW
CARDINAL
SILVER
MOONFLOWER
AQUAMARINE,
(RUBY)

FIRE
HEART, SPINE
MASC.
YELLOW
FIXED
GOLD
MARIGOLD
RUBY (SARDONYX)

EARTH
ABDOMEN
FEM.
YELLOW GREEN
MUTABLE
MERCURY
AZALEA
SAPPHIRE
(SAPPHIRE)
10PM

MIDNIGHT

colors of the spectrum—red, orange, yellow, and so on—were assigned in order, beginning with Aries.

PERSONALITIES. It was believed that temperamentally people belonged to one of three categories: pioneering and forward-looking (cardinal), firm and unchanging (fixed), or changeable (mutable). These characteristics were incorporated into the signs of the zodiac. The astrologers began by assigning cardinal to Aries, fixed to Taurus, mutable to Gemini, and so on, around to Pisces.

METALS. Each of the signs was related to a metal. Aries was iron—strong and unbending; Taurus was copper—hard and polished; Gemini was mercury—quick and shiny.

FLOWERS AND GEMS. Astrologers assigned just about everything to the zodiac, including flowers and gems. Over the centuries, some of these objects have been changed. In parentheses after the names of the original gems are the modern gems now ascribed to the signs.

HOUSES. Ancient astrologers believed that there were twelve compartments—or houses—in a person's life. And each of the houses was ruled by a sign and a planet. The position of the houses and the sign that happened to be in them at the time of one's birth are important to astrologers. The twelve houses that govern a person's life are indicated by the numbers around the center of the circle.

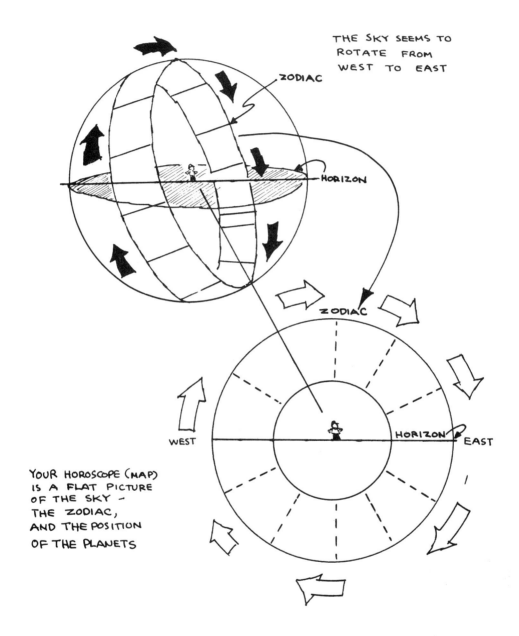

THE SKY SEEMS TO ROTATE FROM WEST TO EAST

ZODIAC

HORIZON

ZODIAC

WEST

HORIZON

EAST

YOUR HOROSCOPE (MAP) IS A FLAT PICTURE OF THE SKY — THE ZODIAC, AND THE POSITION OF THE PLANETS

Casting Your Horoscope

Knowing the day of the week as well as the hour when you were born helps an astrologer to "tell your fortune." And there are many other conditions that he uses. In order to make a forecast, an astrologer prepares a horoscope for you. This is a map of the positions of the sun, moon, and planets at the moment of your birth. Then from the locations and from the way the planets were moving at that time, astrologers predict future events in your life. You can make your own horoscope.

First, draw a circle. Inside it draw a much smaller circle. Divide the larger circle in half by drawing a line across it. This is the horizon. Then divide the circle from top to bottom. The upper end of the line is noon; the lower end is midnight. Divide each of the four sections of the circle into three parts, and draw lines through the center as we have done in the chart on page 36.

Each of the sections between the lines represents two hours.

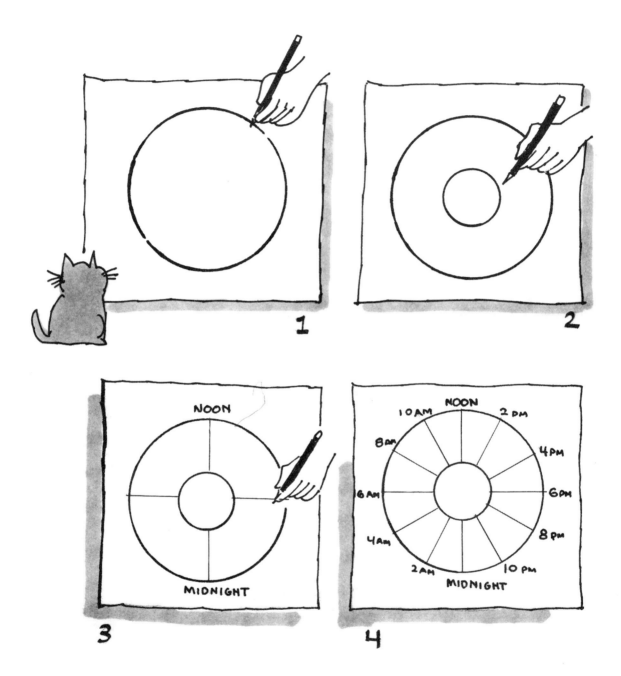

Label each line with the time of day. Begin at the top with noon, then clockwise 2 P.M., 4 P.M., 6 P.M., 8 P.M., and so on.

Find the section of the circle that contains the hour when you were born. Standard time will be more accurate than daylight-saving time. In our example, we have used 1:30 P.M. as the time of birth. Draw the sun symbol in that section.

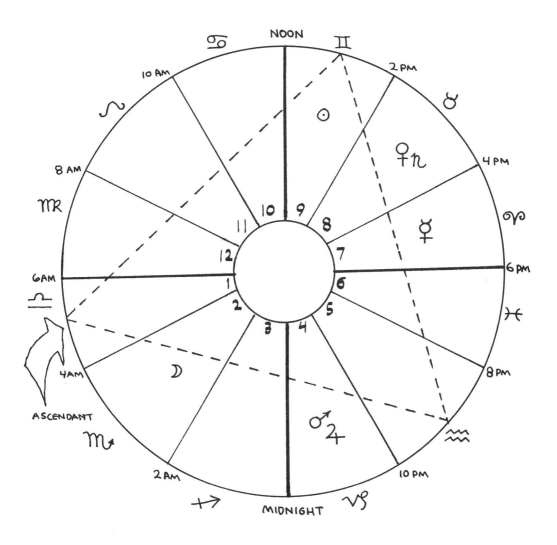

The date of birth gives your sign. Let's say the date was May 26. The sign for that date is Gemini. Draw the symbol for Gemini outside that same section.

Put in the other signs of the zodiac. (You'll find them on page 32). Go counterclockwise, opposite to the direction of the hands of a clock. Start with Gemini, then Cancer, Leo, Virgo, and so on, until you have put in all twelve signs.

The sign in the 4:00–6:00 A.M. section turns out to be Libra. This is your ascendant sign; the sign or constellation that was rising at the time of your birth. Astrologers think this rising sign is very important in casting your horoscope, especially if a planet happened to be in that region of the sky.

Beginning with the ascendant section, number the sections counterclockwise. These numbers are houses. Libra was in house number 1; Gemini, in house number 9. The house locations of the sun, moon, and planets are important to the astrologer.

Each house regulates a division of a person's life. The houses are related to each other by equal-sided triangles. Ancient people attached special meaning to this shape.

If you draw such a triangle, beginning at the center of your ascendant, the other two corners will be in houses numbered 5 and 9. They have special meaning for an astrologer, especially if certain planets happen to be located in them.

For example:

Houses 1, 5, 9   Refer to the body and mind—they tell the
                    astrologer about a person's health.

Houses 2, 6, 10	Refer to the home, to a person's possessions, and what might happen to them.
Houses 3, 7, 11	Refer to a person's family, friends, and relatives.
Houses 4, 8, 12	Refer to sickness and death; the limits that must be placed on everyone; losses.

If the sun, moon, or a planet happens to be in one of the houses, then the house is especially important. For example, if Venus (the planet of love) should be in house 7, special attention should be given to one's very close friends (wife or husband for a married person). Also because of Venus, the person will have unusual artistic ability as a writer, sculptor, painter, musician, or poet. That is because these talents are qualities attributed to Venus.

Your horoscope now contains the signs of the zodiac, the locations of the sun, and the houses.

The next step is to put in the positions of the planets. You cannot do this unless you have planet tables. The astrologer refers to listings of planet positions, similar to ones that an astronomer uses, to find where the planets were at any given moment.

We invented planetary positions for the sample chart, and put the symbols for them in those invented locations. The sun is in house number 9, Jupiter and Mars in house number 4, and so on. The positions of the planets out to Saturn, their houses, and the meanings attached to these positions are below:

| Sun 9 | Possibility of taking a long trip; money may be coming your way even though you don't expect it. |

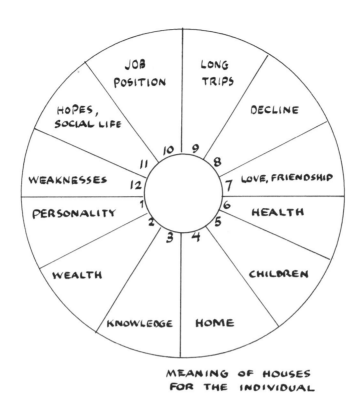

MEANING OF HOUSES
FOR THE INDIVIDUAL

Jupiter 4	Home important in your life; you are a good saver; like to help around the house.
Mars 4	You will probably collect different things; may inherit money; some troubles in the home are likely; perhaps arguments.
Moon 2	You are apt to be extravagant and wasteful; your savings go up and down.
Mercury 7	You should be successful in science or literature; work with a partner will be successful.

Venus 8	For adults there will be great gains (or losses) in marriage or in business; likely to receive an inheritance.
Saturn 8	Big gains will come from hard, steady work; if health is good, long life is likely.

Astrologers get such information from references, some of which were written by Ptolemy, you remember, almost two thousand years ago. There are many other references. Also there are the

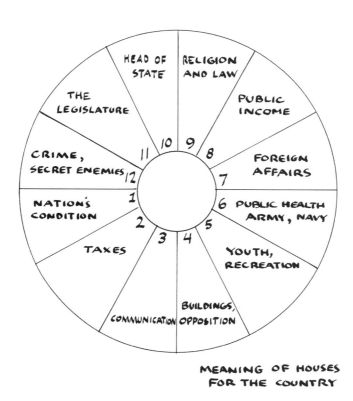

MEANING OF HOUSES
FOR THE COUNTRY

clues in your sky chart, the ones we've already talked about. But there are more. The aspects of the planets, which is the relationship of one planet to another, are additional clues. There are many of them, but these are the principal aspects:

1. Conjunction   When two bodies are together as at the left below, and shown as they would be in a horoscope at the right.

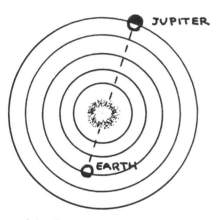

AS SEEN FROM EARTH,
SUN AND JUPITER
ARE TOGETHER

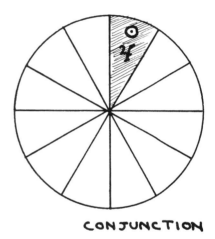

CONJUNCTION

2. Sextile   When two bodies are separated by 60 degrees with earth (the center of your map). The sun and Mercury are in sextile in the chart on page 37—a good omen.

3. Square

When two bodies are separated by 90 degrees—a square corner with the earth. In our example on page 37, Mercury and Mars are in square. This is usually a bad omen.

4. Trine

When two bodies are separated by 120 degrees. This is most favorable; it strengthens the information given by all signs in the houses.

5. Opposition

Two bodies opposite one another—6 signs apart as at the left below, and shown in a horoscope at the right.

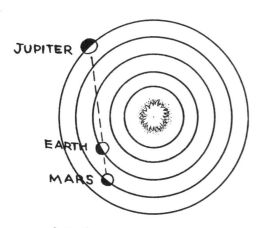

AS SEEN FROM EARTH, JUPITER AND MARS ARE OPPOSITE EACH OTHER

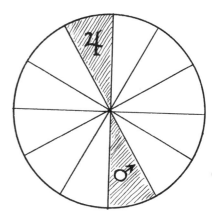

OPPOSITION

The importance that early astrologer-astronomers gave to the aspects of the planets is shown in the writings of Johann Kepler. He was a famous German astronomer who made many discoveries about the orbits of planets. He also practiced astrology and studied how the positions of the planets affected the weather. He kept records of the positions of the planets and the kind of weather that occurred. After eight years this is what he wrote:

If two planets stand at 89 degrees from one another, nothing will happen in the air. But tomorrow, when the full square of 90 degrees is reached, a thunderstorm will suddenly arise. The effect, therefore, does not come from a single star, but from the angle, from the harmonious segment of the circle.

In making an actual horoscope, an astrologer does not place a planet just anywhere in a house. If it were placed roughly, it might

45

vary about thirty degrees from its true location—there are thirty degrees in a house, or in a sign.

Using the seven planets known to the ancients, the twelve signs of the zodiac, and aspects of the planets, an astrologer can cast a horoscope for a person. A horoscope is usually based on one's date and time of birth. But it might be based on the date and time of some special event—the start of a trip, entrance to college, or a person's marriage. Give an astrologer the time and date of the event, and a forecast can be made.

Do objects in the sky really affect our lives? Astrologers say they do. People who do not believe in astrology say they do not.

Do Objects in the Sky Affect Us?

Certainly, everyone agrees that some of the objects in the sky affect us. The sun has the strongest effect on us. Energy from the sun keeps us alive. Plants could not grow without heat and light from the sun. And if there were no plants, we would have nothing to eat. All our food comes from plants, or from animals that eat plants. Wood for heat comes from trees. Oil, gas, and coal come from plants and animals that lived millions of years ago. Electricity comes from heat that can be made by burning oil, gas, and coal. All of our food and energy can be traced back to the sun. Also, the sun is one of the causes of tides.

The main cause of tides is the moon. It is so close to us that the moon's gravitation is strong. It pulls on the earth. The water part of the earth can move, so it piles up at high tide. Differences in the gravitation of the moon on different parts of the earth cause the tides. And the moon affects us in other ways.

Some people say that patients in mental hospitals do not sleep well when there is a full moon. Others say that the moon affects the way plants grow. A long time ago someone wrote a poem that tells how people felt about planting and the appearance of the moon.

Go plant the bean when the moon is light.
And you will find that this is right;
Plant the potatoes when the moon is dark,
And to this line you always hark;
But if you vary from this rule,
You will find you are a fool;
If you always follow this rule to the end,
You will always have money to spend.

Also, many people believe that the moon affects the weather. When the moon is changing from new moon to full, they say there will be pleasant weather. For two weeks after the moon has become full, it will appear a little smaller each night. Many people believe that there will be unpleasant weather during this period—clouds, rain, fog, or snow. Sayings about the moon tell how people think it is related to weather:

Full moon in April brings frost.

Clear moon, frost soon.

The full moon eats clouds.

The moon and weather change together.

48

Or a counter-proverb:

The moon and the weather may change together,
But a change in the moon does not change the weather.

If the moon causes tides, if it affects the weather, then, astrologers say, it can also affect people. And they may be right.

Astrologers also say, if the sun and moon affect us, then the planets affect us, and also the stars. But many people disagree. The stars are too far away, they say. The sun is a star that affects us because it is close by—only about 150 million kilometers away. Light takes about eight minutes to travel from the sun to the earth. The nearest star beyond the sun is very much farther away. It is so far away that light from it takes over four years to reach us. So, even though the stars give off heat and light, very little of it reaches us. If that were not so, there would be no dark nights—starlight would fill the sky at night, just as sunlight fills the sky in daytime.

The planets are much closer to us. They are so close, say astrologers, that they pull on us just as the moon does. That is true. But the pull of the planets on the earth is so small that it cannot be measured. The moon pulls on us because it is so close. The distance from the earth to the moon is about 380,000 kilometers. The distance to Venus when it is nearest to us is still about 35,000,000 kilometers, about a hundred times farther away. Most of the planets are much farther away than Venus. They are so far away that we cannot feel their gravitation.

Also, the planets give off very little energy. The light from the planets comes from the sun. It is sunlight that reflects from the planets, just as moonlight is sunlight that reflects from the moon. Each of the planets gives off some heat. But the amount is very small.

All of these are reasons why astronomers believe the stars and planets do not affect our lives. Astronomers are scientists who study stars and planets and the ways in which they move. Astrologers are not scientists; they are people who interpret the locations and movements of the stars and planets; they use them to forecast what will happen in the future.

Forecasting the future (fortune-telling) by the stars obviously does not work. If it did, calamities could be foretold; astrologers could always win at gambling games (or the stock market); all marriages would be successful, for it would be possible to pick the perfect mate. The stars would dictate our decisions, and the result of every decision, good or bad, would be known ahead of time.

An astrologer uses many of the same tables and charts that are used by an astronomer. Exact positions of the sun, moon and planets, for example, must be found. When the positions are placed on a chart, an astrologer is making a map of the sky as it was at some particular time. In a similar manner, astronomers also make maps of the sky. Their maps look different, but they contain similar information. The big difference is in interpretation. The astrologer believes that the positions of the sun, moon, and planets hold meanings that affect our lives. The astronomer has no such belief. The planets were in these positions, the astronomer agrees. But they had no effect on people who happened to be born at that particular moment.

Modern astrology, you recall, began thousands of years ago with the Chaldeans and Babylonians. They believed that the earth was the center of the universe. They had the geocentric, or earth-centered view. It was impossible for them to explain movements of the seven planets (the sun, moon, Jupiter, Saturn, Mercury, Venus, and Mars) as modern science can. Mystery surrounded them, so it was reasonable for the ancients to consider the seven moving objects as gods.

The priests who had contact with the gods believed they were close by. In Babylonia high pyramids were built in seven steps, using sun dried bricks. Each of the seven steps was dedicated to one of the planet gods, and was the color that the object represented.

Tiles were heat-glazed in the various colors and set in place upon the dried bricks. In some locations the towers were 200 feet high. They were links between heaven and earth. Temples built on the top layers were places where the gods might rest.

Priests who climbed to the top of the tower were close to the gods, and so could communicate with them. From these towers the priests watched the movements of the planets. They saw how steady and even the movements of the sun and the moon were. The other objects moved more unevenly. They were called the "wild goats." They were Mercury, Venus, Mars, Jupiter, and Saturn. They moved in ways unlike the "tame goats," the stars that filled the sky.

The Babylonians and people who lived after them did not know why these planets moved unevenly. It was not until the sixteenth century when Nicholas Copernicus told us that the planets went around the sun that the truth began to be learned.

We see the planets move from west to east in their journey around the sun. But at intervals they seem to stop and then move backward for a while. Then they resume the west-to-east motion. The reason is not because the planets are gods. It is because they move at different speeds around the sun. The inner planets, Mercury and Venus, catch up to us on earth and pass us. And in turn earth catches up to and passes the outer planets. The lines of sight from one planet to another are always changing, and so directions of motion also seem to be changing.

For example, suppose you are on a playground merry-go-round and you're looking at a distant pole. As you go to the right, the pole seems to move to the left. Then as you go to the left, the pole seems to move to the right.

So it is with the earth and Mars, and with all the other planets, too.

Sometimes the planets appeared to be close together, and at

other times far apart. There were occasions when two of them rose, or set, at the same moment. The priests gave special meaning to such events.

Through hundreds of years, astronomers studied these events and the motions that caused them. They learned that the planets did not move around earth. Earth was not the center of everything. It was merely another planet that moved around the sun. It was not a god, nor were the planets. Events in the sky were in no way related to those on earth.

Also, the planets are not near us, as the ancient astrologers believed. The moon is, and it is close enough to cause tides on earth. But the planets are so far away that they cannot affect earth or the people living upon it.

Today we know that all these things are true. Yet many people still believe that the planets influence their lives. They have faith in what their horoscopes tell them.

Tests of this faith have been made many times. One of the tests was conducted by a French scientist. He wanted to know how a horoscope would affect the person receiving it.

He gave the same complete chart to several persons. The chart looked convincing, but it was false. It had nothing to do with the actual positions of the planets. The forecast was a happy one, and so the people were pleased with the chart. The explanations praised them, and also gave them advice that they were glad to follow.

The experiment was not meant to prove that astrology was a fraud, although it may have done so. But it surely showed that astrology depends very much on the ability of an astrologer to convince a person that he can give good advice, whether or not the stars have actually been consulted.

All of us would like to know what the future holds for us. Astrology fascinates many people because they believe that it provides information about future events and helps them to understand themselves and others. They believe this, even though the idea is based upon beliefs of the earth and stars as they were known thousands of years ago—beliefs that have been entirely changed by modern science.

Most scientists agree that astrology is a kind of magic. It is magic based upon the supposed connection between events which in truth are not connected. It is the same as the ancient belief that there are no chance accidents; someone or something purposely causes everything.

Astronomy and astrology developed over the centuries beginning with the ancient Chaldeans and Babylonians. Astronomy became an important science—man's search to understand the universe. Astrology remained magic. Nevertheless, it is still popular. Astrology will continue to be popular as long as people allow themselves to believe in magic rather than in themselves.

Books for Further Reading

Aylesworth, Thomas. *Astrology and Foretelling the Future: A Concise Guide.* Franklin Watts, Inc., 1973.

Gallant, Roy A. *Astrology: Sense or Nonsense?* Doubleday & Co., Inc., 1974.

Helfman, Elizabeth S. *Signs and Symbols of the Sun.* The Seabury Press, Inc., 1974.

Jennings, Gary. *Teenager's Realistic Guide to Astrology.* Association Press, 1971.

Kettelkamp, Larry. *Astrology: Wisdom of the Stars.* William Morrow & Co., Inc., 1973.

Livingston, P. *On Astrology.* Prentice-Hall, Inc., 1974.

McIntosh, Christopher. *Astrology, The Stars and Human Life: A Modern Guide.* Harper & Row, Inc., 1973 (paperback).

Olesky, Walter, and Babbin, Kenneth. *The Universe Is Within You: A Basic Guide to Astrology.* Julian Messner, 1977.

Omarr, Sydney. *Sydney Omarr's Astrological Guide for Teenagers.* New American Library, Inc., 1971 (paperback).

Shapiro, Amy. *Sun Signs: The Stars and Your Life.* Raintree Publishers, Ltd., 1977.

Stearn, Jess. *A Time for Astrology.* Coward, McCann & Geoghegan, Inc., 1971.

Index